Kindle Fire HD 8 & 10 User Guide:
The Complete User Guide With Step-by-Step Instructions. Master Your Kindle Fire HD 8 & 10 in 1 Hour!

Jennifer N. Smith

Table of Contents

Introduction-

The Fire HD is the perfect tablet for the on the go person because it has everything that you need all in one device. You can even add all of your own videos and pictures. On top of this, the Fire HD comes with the use of the Amazon Cloud which means that you will not have to give up your precious space on your Fire HD.

Throughout this book, we are going to learn how you can use your Fire HD, starting with how you can set it up and register it. As we move through the book, we are going to learn all about the apps, transferring your videos and photo and even how you can watch your favorite shows right on your Fire HD.

We are going to learn all about the settings, and how you can personalize your Fire HD and even how you can use your Fire HD with Alexa.

By the time that you finish reading this book, you are going to know everything that you need to know about your Fire HD, how to use it and how to make it work for you.

Chapter 1- Getting To Know Your Fire HD

Before you begin using your Fire HD, it is important for you to get to know the basics. In this chapter, we are going to discuss starting your device, how the controls work, what will happen the first time that you charge your Fire HD, how to register it and more.

Starting the Device

The first time that you turn on your Fire HD you are going to see several screens, welcoming you. You will want to go through each of these screens in order to register your device. We will walk through registering your device in this chapter. In order to turn your device on, you will push the smaller button that is located at the top of the Fire HD and hold it for up to three seconds.

If you want to turn on the sleep mode, you will push the power button once and you will do the same in order to wake up the Fire HD. **In order to turn the device off, you will hold down the power button for three seconds and a prompt will appear on the screen, allowing you to choose to restart, turn off or cancel.**

Battery and Controls

The battery of the Fire HD when fully charged is going to allow for 12 hours of use, which is an upgrade from the 8 hours of the previous version.

On the top of the Fire HD, **you will find a large button,** on the opposite side of the power button. This is where you will adjust the volume. You will also find a **3.5mm headphone Jack** where you can plug in a set of earbuds or headphones.

Near the power button, you will find your charging port. This is where you will plug in your charger. It is important that you are very careful when plugging in and unplugging the charger on any device because if you are rough with the charging cord you can cause damage to the cord or the device.

The device is a touch screen which means that when you tap an option on the screen it is much like clicking the mouse on a computer. You only need to tap the icon one time in order to select it, then wait for it to load. **When you want to scroll, you will swipe your finger across the screen.**

First Time Charging

When you first remove your Fire HD from the box, the tablet should be charged enough for you to go through the set up as well as the registration which we will talk about a little bit later.

You will also notice that your Fire came with a USB cord that will plug into your computer allowing you to charge it. **However, it is important to know that this will take much longer than if you use a wall plug.**

Set Up your Fire HD and Registration

1. After you see the welcome screen, you need to choose your prefer language. Then click continue.

Fire HD 8

Fire HD 10

2. It will be followed by a screen which lists all of the available Wi-Fi connections. Choose which Wi-Fi connection you will use and enter your password if needed.

Fire HD 8

The Complete User Guide With Step-by-Step Instructions. Master Your Kindle Fire HD 8 & 10 in 1 Hour!

Fire HD 10

3. Once you have a Wi-Fi connection, you will move on to the register your device screen. Here you will need to register your device with Amazon. You will need to enter your Amazon account information and if you do not have an account, you will need to choose 'create an account.'

Fire HD 8

Kindle Fire HD 8 & 10 User Guide:

The Complete User Guide With Step-by-Step Instructions. Master Your Kindle Fire HD 8 & 10 in 1 Hour!

Fire HD 10

Register Your Fire

Register your Fire using your existing Amazon account.

Email or mobile number

Amazon password

☐ Hide Password

Forgot password?

New to Amazon?

Start here.

By registering or creating an account, you agree to all the terms found here. Your music will be saved to the Cloud to protect your purchases. The voice features process and retain audio in the Cloud to improve our services.

4. If you do not register your device, you will not be able to make purchases on Amazon.com or access the Kindle Store. As you are registering your device, you are going to need to enter a credit card number as your preferred source of payment. This will allow you to make purchases through Amazon and the Kindle Store.

5. You will also find that on the registration page is an area where you can click to read the terms of service. If you agree to them, click 'I Agree' then you will click the register Continue button.

6. Once this is done, you will be taken to a new screen where you will need to select your time zone. It is important that you select the correct time zone because if you do not, it could lead to issues with you connecting to your Wi-Fi network down the road.

7. The next page will be a page on which you will
   confirm your account information. you will need to
   select the person who will use the Fire HD, in this case
   it will be your Amazon name, you can have the option
   to add your child name here as well, so you can share
   the Fire HD with them and set educational goals and
   time limits. **Then click continue**

Fire HD 8

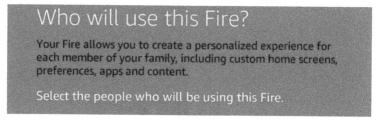

Fire HD 10

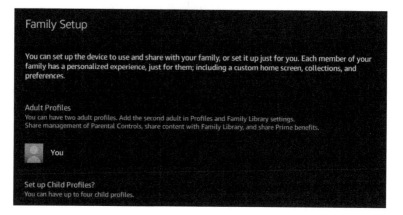

8. Once you have done all of this, you will have the option to link your social media accounts. This is completely optional, however, in order to link your accounts, you will simply click on the social media button that you want to link, input your information and select **"Connect"**

Fire HD 8

Kindle Fire HD 8 & 10 User Guide:

The Complete User Guide With Step-by-Step Instructions. Master Your Kindle Fire HD 8 & 10 in 1 Hour!

Fire HD 10

After that, just click continue to go to the next page, the next screen will ask you to enable your location.

Fire HD 8

Enable Location Services
Allow Maps, other apps, and Amazon to use location and related information.

Learn More

Save Wi-Fi Password to Amazon
Wi-Fi passwords, including those previously entered, will be saved to Amazon to help you connect your other devices

Fire HD 10

Enable Location Services

Allow Maps, other apps and Amazon to use location and related information.
Learn More

When you finished all the set-up, the welcome screen will appear, you can go through the on-screen tutorial now if you want to, or just Exit to start using your Fire HD.

Fire HD 8

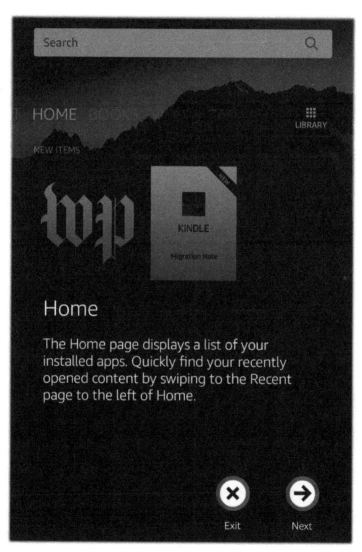

Fire HD 10

Welcome!

This tutorial will guide you through some of the major features and functionality of your new Fire tablet.

Exit   Start

Storage and the Cloud Drive

There are two storage options when it comes to the Fire HD, 16GB, and 32GB. The truth is that either one of these is a fine option because when you purchase the Fire HD, you will receive unlimited storage on the Amazon Cloud Drive, that can be used for the items that you purchase through Amazon.

It is important to know that this Cloud Drive cannot be used for media that you have copied from your computer. So if you do believe that you are going to be copying a lot of media from your computer, the 32GB storage option might be better for you.

What this means is that all of the music, audio, books and movies that you purchase from Amazon, will be stored online instead of on your device for you to use them as you please.

If you know that you are going to be in an area where you are not going to have a connection, you don't have to worry because you can download the media that you want to take with you, use it while you have no connection and then delete it from your device. It will still be available through your cloud.

Learning to Navigate

Let's begin with the navigation bar with is going to appear at the bottom of the screen no matter what app you are using, except when you are reading. If you need to open the navigation bar while you are reading, all that you have to do is to tap the center of the screen and it will appear.

The navigation bar will consist of three buttons which will look like a circle, a triangle and a square.

1. **<u>The circle</u> is going to take you home, or to the previous page that you selected.**

2. **<u>The triangle</u>** is going to take you back to the last screen that you were on.

3. **<u>The square</u>** is going to take you to the task switcher which will allow you to see the apps you have recently used as well as open or close them.

On the home screen, you will see icons which will represent each of the apps you have downloaded or the content that you have purchased. Tapping these icons will take you to that app or to your media.

In order to check your Wi-Fi connection or show the quick settings option, swipe your finger down from the top of the screen and this screen below will appear.

It is important that you take the time to get to know your Fire HD before you begin using it so that if you do find yourself stuck you will know what to do and how you can return to your home menu.

Changing the Wallpaper

If you don't like the original wallpaper on your Fire HD, you can change it.

1. Go to **Setting**, then click on **Display**.

2. You need to select **Wallpaper** and choose the available images that come with your Fire HD from there.

Happy ❷   📶 94% 🔋 10:57

← Display

Wallpaper

Display Brightness
☀️ ————————————————————○

Blue Shade
Adjust the brightness and color of the screen for use before bed.

3. Or you can use your own images by clicking on **Pick Image Icon**.

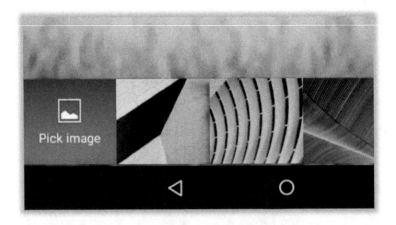

Chapter 2- Available Settings

Understanding the available settings is very important when it comes to using your Fire HD. In order to access these settings, you will want to swipe down from the top of the screen. This is not only going to give you access to the quick settings, but it is also going to give you access to the more advanced settings on your Fire HD.

OR click on the Setting Icon on the home page.

Quick Actions

The first thing that I want to go over with you are the quick actions that you can do simply by swiping down from the top of your screen.

1. The first setting is the auto-rotate option. This setting will allow you to lock or unlock the auto-rotation of the screen. If you want the screen to automatically rotate, you will turn this option on, on the other hand, if you do not want to screen to rotate, you can switch this to off.

2. The brightness setting is going to allow you to adjust the brightness of your screen. The higher you set this setting the brighter your screen will be.

3. The wireless setting is going to allow you to connect to a Wi-Fi network.

4. Airplane mode setting is to take it on and off.

5. Do not disturb setting is to mute all of your notification.

6. The Help setting is going to put you into contact with an Amazon Customer Service Agent who will help you with any issue that you are facing as well.

7. The Settings option is going to take you into the more advanced settings.

8. Blue Shade setting is to turn the blue shade on or off.

9. Camera setting allows you to turn the camera on.

More Advanced Settings

Once you choose the Settings Option, you are going to be able to go into the more advanced settings on your Fire HD.

1. The wireless option is going to enable you to connect to a Wi-Fi network and it is also going to enable you to turn the airplane mode on and off.

2. My Account setting will allow you to connect to social networks as well as manage the accounts that are associated with the device. This is where you will change your preferred payment source as well.

3. Profiles and Family Library is the setting which will allow you to add profiles for the other members in the house. When you do this, each member can have a personalized carousel, collections, apps and content. This is a great option if there are children that are going to be using the device.

4. "Sync Device" setting which is going to allow you to sync your device and check for any updates.

5. The Device Options Setting is going to allow you to update your device, back up the content that you have on your device, view the free storage space on the device, change the date and the time that is displayed on your device and change the name of your device.

6. The Power Management Setting is going to enable you to manage your battery usage.

← Power

Battery: 93% (Charging)

Smart Suspend

Automatic Smart Suspend
Increase standby battery life by automatically turning off wireless connectivity when you aren't using your
Fire.

Scheduled Smart Suspend
Increase standby battery life by turning off wireless connectivity during scheduled times.

Schedule

Advanced

Display Settings
Reduce display brightness, or choose a lower display sleep time to preserve battery life.

Wireless Settings
Disable Wi-Fi, Bluetooth, or Location based services to preserve battery life.

7. The Display and Sound Setting is going to enable you to adjust the brightness of the screen, adjust your volume and it is going to allow you to adjust the mirroring settings.

8. The Keyboard and language setting is going to enable you to change the language of the device as well as the keyboard and it is also going to enable you to choose the voice for the text to speech setting.

9. The Parental Controls are going to enable you to turn the parental controls both on and off, and you will be able to manage the profiles for the children in your home.

Happy   📶 46% 🔋 4:50

← Parental Controls

Household Profiles
Manage profile settings for child profiles in Household.

Parental Controls
Set a password to restrict purchasing, content types, web browsing, and access to other features. Access to Alexa is blocked when Parental Controls are enabled.

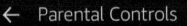

All about Bluetooth Pairing

You can pair your Fire HD via Bluetooth with other devices or accessories. In order to make Bluetooth pairing easier, you need to make sure before you get started that the device or accessory that you are trying to pair with is within range of your Fire HD.

Begin by turning on Bluetooth for both of the devices and ensure that pairing has been enabled. In order to do this on your Fire HD, Go on setting on your home page and choose the 'wireless'. From there, you will choose, 'Bluetooth.'

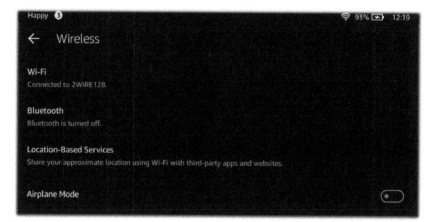

Tap on to enable your Bluetooth. This will allow your Fire HD to search for other devices that are available. Under the list of available devices, choose the device that you want to pair your Fire HD with.

You will have to allow both of the devices to pair and then you are done.

Special Features

The mirroring feature (For Only Fire HD 10) is going to allow you to display what is on your Fire HD on your television or another compatible device. This can be done by pairing your device with the Fire HD or via an **HDMI** dongle if your Fire HD is not able to find the device.

The first thing that you need to do when you are using the mirroring feature is to ensure that your device is discoverable to your Fire HD. If you are unsure how to make your device discoverable, you will need to look in your owner's manual.

On your Fire HD, you will want to swipe down from the top of the screen and tap the settings option. From here, you will choose the display and sounds option and then the display mirroring option.

This will cause your Fire HD to look for any devices that are within range that are compatible. Find the name of your device that you want to connect with and tap on it. The first time that you connect with a device, it could take up to 30 seconds.

In order to stop the mirroring, simply swipe down on your Fire HD screen and tap 'stop mirroring'.

← Display

Wallpaper

Display Brightness

Blue Shade
Adjust the brightness and color of the screen for use before bed.

Display Sleep
After 5 minutes of inactivity

Font Size
Normal

When Device is Rotated
Rotate the contents of the screen

Display Mirroring
Mirror your Fire's display to an external display.

Chapter 3- The Internet and Your Device

Not only are you able to read all of your favorite Kindle books on your Fire HD, or mirror your favorite shows onto your television, but you can also use the internet on your Fire HD, just like you would on your laptop!

Internet Browser

Silk is the name of the internet browser that you will use on your Fire HD. Many people have asked why Amazon didn't just choose to use one of the existing browsers. Amazon has answered that by stating that by creating their own browser that used Amazon's servers, they were able to ensure faster service to their customers.

The Silk icon will be located on your home page. In order to search for a website, simply type what you are searching for in the search bar and tap the search button.

On the options bar, you will also find a home icon, back and forward icons, icon, a menu icon and a favorites icon.

Silk works just like most of the browsers that you would use on your laptop or computer as it uses tabs, which will enable you to have more than one web page open at a time and the switching between these tabs.

If you want to bookmark a site when you are using the Silk browser, you will click on **Three Dots icon**, then tab on Add Bookmark. After you click this tab, a dialog box will appear where you can either cancel or bookmark the page. In order to delete a booked marked page, you will tap on **Menu icon** (Three Lines icon), then tap on the bookmark which will display a thumbnail of all of the pages you have bookmarked. Hold down on the page you want to delete. A menu will appear and all you have to do is tap the remove bookmark option.

If you are looking for a specific topic, within a page and do not want to read the entire page, click the three dots icon that is located in the options bar. A list of options will appear on the screen and you will choose, 'find in page.'

Tap on 'find in page' then type in what you are searching for. If what you are looking for is located within the page, you will be taken directly to it.

In order to view your browsing history, you will click the menu icon (Three Lines) that is located at the top of your screen on the Silk browser. From here, you will tap the history button and then you can choose whether you want to see the history from today or the past seven days. If you see a web page that you want to visit, simply tap on it.

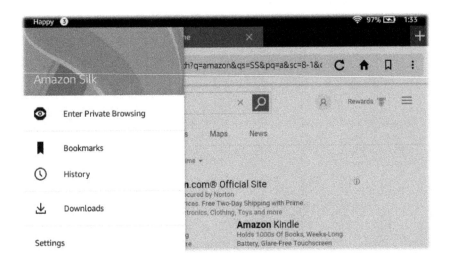

Setting Up Your Email

In order to set up your email account on your Fire HD, you will have to have an already established email account from an online provider such as AOL or Gmail.

Just tab on Email icon on your home page, then you can add your email account by input your email information.

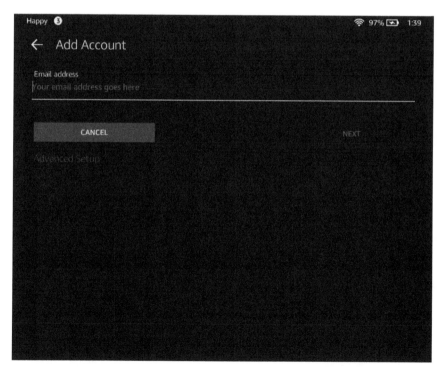

Next, you will tap the save option and if you want to view

your inbox, simply tap the view inbox option. You can set up as many email accounts as you want on your Fire HD.

How To use the Calendar

When you first open the calendar, you are going to see a completely empty calendar. At the top of your screen, you will see a tab which will allow you to choose how you want your calendar displayed... Day, week, or month.

Sun	Mon	Tue	Wed	Thu	Fri	Sat
29	30	31	1	2	3	4
5	6	7	8	9	10	11
12	13	14	15	16	17	18
19	20	21	22	23	24	25
26	27	28	1	2	3	4
5	6	7	8	9	10	11

If you want to add an event to your calendar, you just need to click on **(the green add sign),** next the Sync Amazon Cloud Calendar screen will pop up. It lets you know that Amazon Cloud Calendar events will be synchronized across Amazon devices and services. At this point, if you accept it then click on Accept. If you do not want to do that then click on Setting, this will allow you to disable synchronization.

Now you're almost done, next screen is the screen that allows you to add an event to your calendar.

What About Contacts?

The contacts app is pre-installed on the Fire HD and you can access it by tapping on the app's icon which is found on your home screen. From there, you will simply tap on the contacts app.

If you have already set up an email account, you can import all of your contacts from your associated email account. After you set up the email account and open up the contacts, a message will pop up on the screen asking you if you want to import your contacts.

If you want to add a new contact, simply tap the 'add contact' option and you will find fields for the name, address, phone number and email address for your new contact.

First name

Last name

Phonetic last name

Phonetic first name

Nickname

CHANGE

Phone   Mobile

Tap on whatever field you wish to fill in and use the keyboard to fill in the information. If you want to add a photo, tap the photo icon on the side of the contact information. From here you can choose where you want to add the photo from. Tap the source that you want to get the photo from and when you are done, you will want to make sure that you click the save button.

Having not only the ability to browse the internet but take advantage of all of the other features mentioned in this chapter is one of the reasons that the Fire HD has become so popular. No longer are you restricted to just reading Kindle books, but the Fire HD can now do all of the same things that your other devices can do. It is an all in one tablet.

Chapter 4 - All about Apps

Now we are going to talk about how you can download apps and games from the app store. When you purchase an app or game from the Amazon App Store you will have the 1-click purchase option, or you can use a gift card or Amazon coins to make your purchase.

In order to use the 1-click purchase option, you will have to have a credit or debit card on record as your preferred source of payment.

How to Download Apps and Game

There are also free apps and games which you can download if they are available to your country. On your Fire HD, there will be an Amazon App Store app already installed.

Just simply select it, then you can choose the apps and

games that you want to download.

Once you have your choice, then go ahead and click the GET button, Next click on download. Once it finished download, this app icon will show up on your home screen. Now you can enjoy your app or game.

Top 5 Essential Free Apps for Your Fire HD

1. Evernote

Evernote is a free note taking app, you can sync your notes to your online account, you can access your notes from anywhere. If you like, you can organize the different section of the notes into a notebook.

2. Cozi Family Organizer

You and your family can use this app to create journal, to-do lists and shopping lists that the whole family can access it. If one family member deletes the item in the shopping list, this will show on everyone else's app.

3. BeFunky

This is one the best photo editor apps available and it's free to use. There are lots of photo effects that you can use such as overlays, frames, sticker and more. Of course, you can do the basic things like sharpen, crop and rotate your photos.

4. CCleaner

Cleaning your Fire HD frequently can help it running like new, it removes junk, reclaims disk space and monitors your system so the device can run smoothly.

5. AccuWeather

This is the best free app for weather forecast. The interface looks nice and easy to use. You can get minute by minute local weather forecast, severe weather alerts and what I like the best is the 15 days weather forecast, this allows you to plan your day accordingly.

Learning to Uninstall Apps and Games

Now that you know how to download apps, it is also important for you to know how to uninstall apps and games. There are two different ways for you to uninstall apps and games from your Fire HD.

The first way for you to uninstall an app is for you to hold your finger on the icon until a menu pops up which will give you the option to uninstall the app.

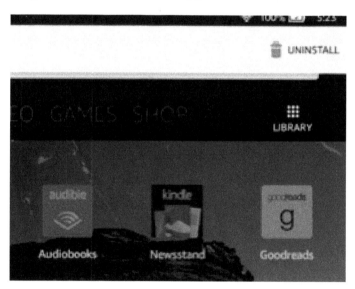

While that is the easiest way to uninstall an app, it does not always uninstall the app completely. If this happens, there is a second method which will allow you to ensure that the app is completely uninstalled.

First, go to your SETTING, then tap on App and Game.

Next you will need to go to Manage All Application, all your apps and games will appear here.

Now find app or game you want to remove, then tap on it and other screen will pop up. This is the screen which tell you all of the app's information and include the **UNINSTALL option**. The last step is to click on uninstall, then this app or game will completely remove from your Fire HD.

Features for Everyone in the Family

Not only is the Fire HD great for you, but it is great for the entire family, kids included! Because kids today enjoy spending time on devices, the Fire HD can make reading fun for them again. It is great for kids because it is so easy to use and it offers parental controls to ensure that no matter what is downloaded, your child is safe and that they can only view content that is appropriate for their age.

Amazon offers an app called Free Time which focuses on children and educating them while they are still having fun. One of the great features about the Free Time app is that in order for your child to exit it, you have to enter a password which means that you will know exactly what they are doing while they are on the Fire HD.

However, the best thing about the Free Time app is that it allows you to set a time limit as to how long your child will be allowed to watch videos, play games and so on.

Of course, there are many different apps available for your

Fire HD. It can be used to play games, watch videos, and of course read. It is finally the Kindle Fire that we have all been waiting for. The Kindle Fire that is not just for Kindle books, but is for everything that we do each day.

Amazon FreeTime

Get started in **3** simple steps:

1 Add a profile.

2 Fill it up with content.
   You can add books and apps you already own. Learn More

3 Create a password.

GET STARTED

Chapter 5- Reading On Your Fire HD

Of course, when you are using the Fire HD, you are going to be able to access and read all of the Kindle books that you love as well as all of the digital media you can absorb through the newsstand. The Kindle was originally created for Kindle book readers, but over the years, it has evolved into an amazing tablet that offers many features. However, I feel that it is very important for us to cover how to access your books and the newsstand on your Fire HD.

How to Buy and Read Your Books

Purchasing books and other media on your Fire HD is very simple. Beginning at the home screen, tap the Book or the Newsstand Icon, depending on which you want to purchase.

Then to go store by tapping on the Shopping Cart icon on the top right corner.

Scroll through and find what it is that you want to purchase. Once you have found what you want to purchase, tap on it. If you are purchasing a magazine or newspaper, you will tap the subscribe button.

If you are purchasing a book, you can preview the book to ensure that it is exactly what you are looking

for. Tap 'Download Sample' in order to see a preview. You will have to purchase the book in order to view the entire thing.

Once you decide that you want to purchase the book, tap the buy icon. After you purchase a book or magazine, it will automatically download to your Fire HD and it will also be stored in the cloud. After you have read it, you can delete it from your Fire HD and it will still be stored in the cloud.

Accessing Free eBooks On Amazon

There are tons of free eBooks available on Amazon. The reason for this is because when an author first publishes a book, they are trying to get it in front of readers, therefore, they run promotions, giving the book away for free or at a reduced price. The authors are able to run these promotions every three months, which means a lot of free books are available all of the time.

In order to access these free eBooks, all you have to do is type in the subject or genre that you want to read about, then sort the price from low to high. If you do not have Kindle Unlimited, this is a great way for you to get plenty of eBooks and it is also a great way for you to decide if you want to purchase Kindle Unlimited.

If you do have Kindle Unlimited, all of the eBooks are free for you to read with is wonderful. This will allow you to access books written by all of your favorite authors for one low rate each month.

Reading Basics

While you are reading your books or media from the newsstand, you will swipe your screen from right to left to turn the page. If you have to stop reading, don't worry, the Fire HD will automatically bookmark the page that you are on then when you go back to reading you will begin on the last page that you were reading before you were interrupted.

You can also read and listen to your books at the same time as well as highlight the areas which are important to you or that you want to come back to later. In order to highlight while using the Fire HD, you will hold your finger down on the area that you want to highlight, then the highlighter icon will appear and you will tap it.

If you come across a word that you do not know, the Fire HD is going to automatically provide you with the definition of it, you also can translate it to other languages, and Fire HD also provide you with a short information from Wikipedia.

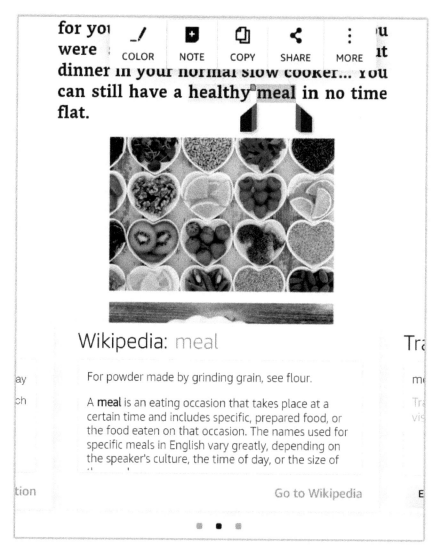

for you ... you
were ... it
dinner in your normal slow cooker... You
can still have a healthy meal in no time
flat.

_/	■	⬜	<	⋮
COLOR	NOTE	COPY	SHARE	MORE

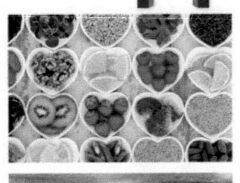

Dictionary   Wi

meal ¹ /mēl/ n. any of the regular occasions in a day   Fo

when a reasonably large amount of food is eaten, such   A

as breakfast, lunch, or dinner.   ce
                                                           th
                                                           sp
                                                           th

Change Dictionary   Full Definition

If you want to add a bookmark, tap on the center of the screen and you will see the icon bookmark on the right hand corner. To add the bookmark, simply tap the icon.

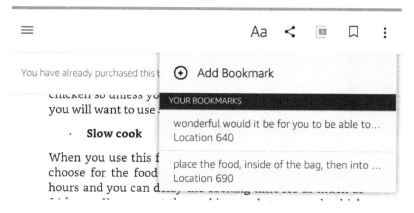

In order to add a note, simply tap on the text that you want to highlight (drag your finger if it is more than one word) and then tap the 'note' option.

You will type in your note, and tap save. If you want to edit the note, tap the icon where the note appears, then tap edit. After you have made the changes that you want to make, simply tap save. In order to delete a note, tap the note icon then tap delete. A dialog box will appear and you will tap delete again.

The Fire HD makes reading eBooks a delight as well as easy. It is wonderful to be able to access all of your favorite titles without having shelves full of books taking up space in your house and gathering dust.

Reading Your Kindle eBook- 2 Helpful Features

1. <u>**Word Wise**</u> is a feature that you will use while you are reading your Kindle books. You may notice on the product pages of some Kindle books that Word Wise is enabled. **When you use this feature, it will automatically detect words that are not commonly used and display hints on the page as to the meaning of the word**.

This will make it easier for you to continue reading the books that you purchase without having to click on a word or open up the dictionary in another window. However, if you do want to see the full definition, you can click on the hints and the definition will be provided for you.

(For Fire HD 8): To turn Word Wise on and off, just simply tab on the center of your Kindle Book page. And on the top right corner, you will see the three dots stacked icon, just click on it and choose additional setting. it will bring you to the screens that allow you to turn it on or off.

← Reader Settings

Language Learning

Word Wise
Enable Word Wise in books

Notifications

Push Notifications sent to this device

WORD WISE

Word Wise
Show hints above challenging words when available

Show Multiple-Choice Hints
When we're unsure of the correct hint for a word, we'll show you a list of possible meanings and ask you to pick the one that is most helpful.

(For Fire HD 10) In order to turn Word Wise on and off, just simply tab on the center of your Kindle Book page. And on the top of your right hand side you will see the three dots stacked icon, now just click on it and it will show Word Wise. Next you need to click on it, and it will bring you to the screen that allow you to turn it on or off.

Now include The 250 Best Echo Easter Eggs

Jennifer N. Smith

2. Word Runner is a feature that is supposed to help you read faster because it displays one word at a time in the center of your screen. This feature will only work for books that have been written in English and it is not available with all titles.

In order to turn Word Runner on, while you are reading, you will tap the center of the page a menu icon will appear that will look like three dots stacked on top of each other. Tap that icon and then choose Word Runner. From here, you will be able to choose how many words per minute you want to be displayed with options ranging from 100 words a minute to 900 words a minute.

If you want to pause the Word Runner, simply hold your finger on the middle of the screen. While Word Runner is paused, you can swipe left or right to manually go through the words. When you are ready to start again, tap the center of the screen and the Word Runner will pick back up on the word displayed on the screen.

There are many different features available on the Fire HD and it is important that you take the time to learn about them and try them so that you know you are getting the most out of your Fire HD as possible.

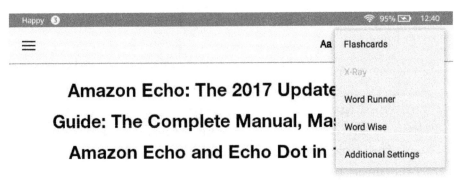

Aa   Flashcards

X-Ray

Word Runner

Word Wise

Additional Settings

Amazon Echo: The 2017 Update Guide: The Complete Manual, Master Amazon Echo and Echo Dot in

Now include <u>The 250 Best Echo Easter Eggs</u>

Jennifer N. Smith

← Word Runner

- Echo Will Transform Your Child's Bedtime Routine

Chapter 5- Echo Skills

- Most recently Added Echo Skills

Chapter 6- Amazon Echo, Troubleshooting

Chapter 7- Streaming Your Favorite Music On Echo

Chapter 8- How To Use Echo For Your Business Or Job

Chapter 9- Creating A Smart Home With Echo

Chapter 10- Helpful Echo Tips and Tricks

Bonus Chapter- The 250 Best Echo Easter Eggs You Can Ask

Conclusion-

Introduction

Personal assistants play a huge role in many of our lives, ensuring that we do not miss our appointments, know when projects are due and even help

↺　　　▶　　　↻

Words Per Minute

100　　　　　　　500　　　　　　　900

Chapter 6- How to Purchase and Listen to Audio

The Fire HD comes with Amazon music already preinstalled which means that in order to access Amazon music, all you have to do is tap on the icon in order to download music, play music or purchase music. **If you have an Amazon Prime membership, you can add your selected songs to a playlist, for free.**

Adding Music

In order to add music from Amazon to your Fire HD, you will simply select the music that you want to add from Amazon music and tap the icon that looks like a plus sign.

If you push the play button while you are in the Amazon Music store, you will only hear a sample of the song, the entire song is not going to be played. In order to listen to the entire song, you will need to add it to your music library.

What about importing your music from another source? Many people already have music on other devices such as their laptops or computers and they want to transfer that music to their Fire HD so that they do not have to repurchase it. If you want to do this, don't worry, it is quite simple to do.

It does not matter if you are trying to import music that has been purchased on iTunes or that has been ripped from your CDs, you will import it all the same way. However, it is important to know that you are only allowed to import 250 songs for free. After the first 250 songs, you will have to pay 24.99 per year to import up to 250,000 songs.

There are a few different ways for you to import music from your laptop or computer to your Fire HD.

1. The first way that I want to talk about is transferring your music by using a micro-USB cable. Begin by connecting both devices via the micro-USB cable. Once the two are connected, you will want to unlock the screen on your Fire HD. Once you have unlocked the screen the computer or laptop is going to recognize that the Fire HD is connected to it.

Open your File Explorer and look under THIS PC/COMPUTER and you will find the Fire HD listed as Fire or Kindle. Highlight your music that you want to import onto the Fire HD and holding down the left mouse button, drag it to the Kindle or Fire folder and put it under the music folder, dropping it there.

This will upload your music to the cloud and it will be available through the music app on your Fire HD.

2. The second way for you to import music from a computer or laptop. From the device that contains the music that you want to import to the Fire HD, go to the Amazon Music website. On the left of the screen, you will see the option, 'upload your music'. Click it. This will install the Amazon Music app onto your computer.

Next, you will choose, "Your library" which is located at the top of the screen. Then look for "View the music on your computer" and click there. Now you will be able to right click on any of the music that is on your computer and upload it. Again, this will be uploaded to the cloud and will be available through the music app on your Fire HD.

How to Listen to Your Music

Now that you know how to get music onto your Fire HD, it is important for you to know how to actually listen to that music. The first thing that you will want to do is to find the Music icon on the home screen and tap it.

Next, you will locate the music in your library that you want to listen to. Tap the song that you want to hear. If you tap the first song in a playlist, the Fire HD will play the entire playlist for you.

At the bottom of the screen, you will see the controls which you can use. These are previous, pause/play, next, shuffle and restart and Volume.

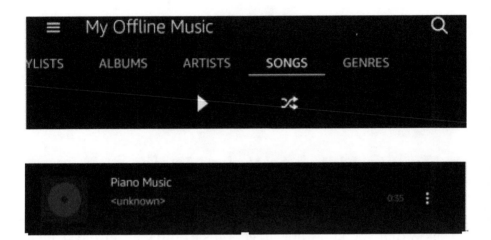

How to Listen to Audiobooks

One of the great things about Kindle books is getting to listen to them, these are known as Audiobooks. From the Audiobooks library that is found on your Fire HD, you will be able to purchase audiobooks, browse audiobooks and listen to audiobooks.

From the home screen, you will look for the Audiobooks Icon. In order to browse or purchase audiobooks, you will click on the shop option and find the book that you want to purchase. If you tap the title you will be able to listen to a sample of the book, however, you must purchase the book in order to listen to it in its entirety.

If you want to listen to one of your audiobooks, swipe to the left side of the screen and tap on the audiobooks option. Here, your audiobooks will be listed. Simply tap on the audiobook that you want to listen to and it will be downloaded.

Once the audiobook is downloaded, you will be able to listen to the book, whether or not the Fire HD is connected to the internet.

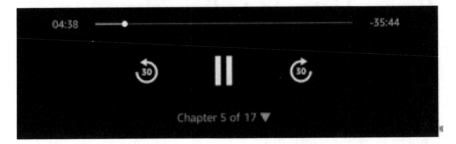

You can earn badges which are based off of the amount of time that you spend listening. All of this is located under your Stats and Badges. From your home screen, simply tap on the audiobooks option then you will tap on menu then the stats/badges option. **It is here that you will be able to see your daily, weekly and monthly stats as well as your badges.**

If you want to link your Amazon and your Audible accounts, go to audible.com and log in using your audible information. After you log in, you will be asked if you want to link your accounts, simply click 'link now'.

You will be asked for your audible password, then your Amazon email and password. You will then select your default payment.

After you have done this, your Audible audiobooks are going to appear on your Fire HD. It is important to note that from this point forward when you go to your Audible account, you will use your Amazon email and password to log in as the previous email and password will no longer work.

How to Manage Your Audio

All of your audio files are going to be stored on the Amazon cloud. However, when you download, for example an audiobook to your Fire HD, you will be able to listen to it without Wi-Fi access. After you are done listening to the audio, you can delete it from your Fire HD without deleting it from your cloud. This means that you will never have to repurchase it.

While I do want to focus on managing your audio, I also

want to focus on managing all of your storage. All of the digital purchases that you make from Amazon are going to be stored on the Amazon cloud which will allow you to download them over and over again.

The reason for this is so that all of the storage on your device is not used up by the purchases that you make. One way to ensure that you are not wasting your storage is to delete the digital purchases from your device after you are done with them. Since these purchases are stored in the cloud, if you want to access them later, they will be there without taking up storage on your Fire HD.

If you want to remove digital purchases from your Fire HD and store them in the cloud all you have to do is go to **settings>storage**.

Here you will be able to archive items that have not been used recently to free up as much space as you need to on your device.

It is important for you to know that if your child is using the Free Time app, all of the items that you have downloaded to the child's profile such as books will take up storage space on your Fire HD. In order to remove some of these digital purchases from the Free Time app, simply tap on the item that you want to remove and hold your finger on the item until a dialog box pops up. Next, you will simply click 'Uninstall'. Remember, even if you delete it from your device, it will be stored in the cloud for you to access later.

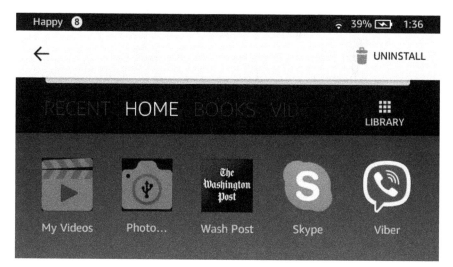

Playing Music on Other Devices

Of course, just because we have all of our music on our Fire HD, it does not mean that we only want to listen to our music on our Fire HD. So before we finish up with this chapter, I want to talk a little bit about accessing your music from other devices.

You can play your music back from the cloud on all of your devices or you can download the music from the cloud to your devices. All you have to do is to log into your Amazon account from your device to access the cloud and choose what a music or other audio you want to listen to or download.

Being able to keep all of your digital media and audio on the cloud is a great way for you to save a ton of storage space on your Fire HD. No other device gives you this option but thanks to Amazon, you will never run out of storage space for all of your digital purchases.

Chapter 7- How to Watch Videos

Did you know that you can watch videos on your Fire HD? Not only can you watch videos, but you can purchase them, rent them and even stream them to your television! In this chapter, I want to talk about how you can take advantage of these features.

How to Watch YouTube Videos

It's simple to watch YouTube Videos on your Fire HD, just tab on the Silk browser on your home screen and go to YouTube website. Then you can watch any video which you want to watch.

Relaxing Music for Stress Relief. Healing Music for Meditaion, Soothing for Massage, Deep Sleep, Spa

How To Open and Play Videos

Starting on the Fire HD home screen, you will want to find the Videos icon and tap it. Next click on the menu icon (three lines) which located on top left hand corner and go to Video Library.

This will display all of the videos that you have rented, that have not expired, as well as all of the videos that you have purchased. You will be given the option of watch now or download. If you choose the watch now option and have already started watching the video previously, then choose the resume option.

How can you buy or rent videos? In order to access the videos, you have to purchase them or rent them. In order to do this, you will have to have a valid 1-click payment method set up. However, **Prime TV and videos can be watched at no additional charge.** If you are a Prime member, meaning that you have previously signed up for Prime and paid the yearly subscription fee, you can access tons of videos and television shows completely free.

Jennifer N. Smith

If you are renting a video, you will pay a specified amount which will allow you access to the video for a specific amount of time.

From the home screen, you will tap the Videos icon, then search for the movie or televisions show that you want to watch. If you know what you want to watch, simply tap the magnifying glass and type the name into the search bar.

If you are browsing in the store, simply swipe from the left side of your screen to look for movies or television shows. Once you have found what you want to watch, you will tap the rent or buy button and the purchase will automatically be billed to whatever account you chose as your 1-click method of payment.

After you purchase or rent your video, you can either stream it and watch it right then or you can download it and watch it later with no Wi-Fi necessary.

How to Transfer Your Own Videos To Your Fire HD

Transferring your own videos to your Fire HD is not as complicated as it may sound. The first thing that you will need to do is to connect your computer to your Fire HD via a Micro-USB cable. Unlock the screen on your Fire HD, allowing your computer to recognize that the two are connected.

On your computer, you will open the file explorer and find where Kindle or Fire is listed. It is important for you to know where this is because this is where you will be placing the videos.

Next, highlight the videos that you want to transfer and drag them to the Kindle or Fire under Movies folder. It will take your computer a few seconds depending on how many files you want to transfer. After you transfer these to the Fire HD, they will be located in the cloud, however you will be able to download them to your device just as you would any other media.

Watch Your Movies On Your TV

One of the great things about the Kindle Fire HD is not only that you can purchase and rent movies, but you can watch them on your television as well!

The first way that you can play the movies on your television is via an **HDMI cable**. To begin, you will need an HDMI cable with a standard **USB connecto**r at one end and a **micro-HDMI connector** at the other. If you want to keep your Fire HD near you, enabling you to use the Fire HD as a remote, you will need a long enough cord to reach from your television to where you will be sitting.

It is important for you to know that this is only going to work if you have a television which had an HDMI port. If your television does not support HDMI don't worry, we will get to that in a few minutes.

It is also important for you to understand that this is only going to work if you are using the Kindle Fire HD. Earlier versions of the Kindle and the HDX are not going to be able to be used with this method.

Begin by plugging the standard HDMI end of your HDMI cord into an HDMI port into your television. Plug the micro-HDMI end of the cord into your Fire HD.

Switch your television to the HDMI input. The way that you will do this will vary depending on your television. If you do

95

not know how to switch to the HDMI input on your television, refer to your owner's manual.

It is important for you to make sure that your Fire HD is turned on before you switch to your HDMI input because if not, the television is not going to recognize the connection.

The Fire HD screen should pop up on your screen within a few seconds of switching to the HDMI input. If this does not happen, you need to check the connection. Make sure that the HDMI cord is properly connected to both the television and the Fire HD. If this does not help, make sure that you have chosen the correct HDMI input.

This is all there is to it. Now you can play the video on your Fire HD, just as you normally would and the video will simultaneously play on your television as well. You can also use streaming video apps such as Netflix, and Hulu on your Kindle Fire HD and stream them to your television this way as well.

What if you do not have an HDMI television?

Don't worry, even if you have a non-HDMI television, you can still watch the videos on your Fire HD on the television.

The first thing that you are going to need to do is to grab some supplies. You will need an HDMI cable and a converter box.

It is important that you purchase a converter box that is labeled as HDMI to AV Composite Video + Audio Converter. It is also important that you purchase an HDMI cord that has the standard HDMI connector at one end and the micro-HDMI on the other.

Begin by plugging the HDMI cord into your Fire HD and the converter box. Then plug the converter box into your television.

Make sure that your Fire HD is on and then switch your television to the proper input. The Fire HD screen should appear on your television and you can now play the video on your Fire HD. It will play on the television at the same time.

Alternatively, if you have a smart television, you can use the mirroring feature to play the videos on your television. In order to do this, you have to first ensure that your TV is discoverable to your Fire HD.

On the fire HD will swipe down from the top of the screen and choose the settings option. Next, you will tap the display option. Then choose display mirroring. Here you will find a list of discoverable devices. Tap the name of your television then your fire HD will connect. It can take up to 20 seconds for the device's screen to show on your television. In order to stop mirroring simply tab stop mirroring.

Chapter 8-All about your Camera and Documents

The fire HD comes with a front-facing camera that can be used for video calls, but it can also be used to take pictures and record personal videos.

It's important to know that all of the photos that you take with the fire HD are going to be uploaded to the cloud automatically.

In order to stop this from happening, you will need to tap the menu icon, while you are in the photos library in then to settings. Here you'll see that option to turn automatic uploads on or off.

← Photos Settings

Auto-Save
Automatically save and secure your photos and videos to Amazon Cloud Drive. You can save at any other time by tapping the upload button on an image.

Photos

Videos

Only When Charging
Upload only when connected to a charger

Transferring Photos

You can transfer your photos from your Fire HD to your computer and vice versa. You will need to connect your Fire HD and your computer via a USB cable.

You will need to make sure that you unlock the screen on your Fire HD so that your computer will recognize it. Next, you will look under the computer folder and look for the Fire or Kindle folder. It is important for you to know where this is because if you are transferring to your Fire HD, this is where you will drop the files.

Now, let's focus only on transferring the photos from your computer to your Fire HD. Begin by selecting the photos that you want to transfer.

If you want to transfer more than one photo, you can hold down the CTRL button as you select the photos. Drag the photos to the Fire or Kindle folder and drop them in the photos section. It will take your computer a few seconds to a few minutes to transfer the files depending on how many you are transferring.

Before you do this, you need to know that these photos are going to be loaded straight to the cloud. If you do not want your photos loaded to the cloud you should not transfer them to the Fire HD without turning off the automatic upload. **I**

explained how to do this earlier.

In order to transfer pictures to your computer from your Fire HD, you will want to click on the Fire or Kindle folder that is located under the computer folder. Select the photos that you want to transfer using the same method mentioned above and drop them into whatever folder you want them to be located in on your computer.

It really is as simple as that when it comes to transferring your photos to and from your Fire HD.

Learning to Work With Documents

One app that you will notice on your home screen is the Docs Library. This is where all of your documents are going to be stored. It is possible for you to save your favorite documents to the home screen and you can also save documents to the Amazon cloud.

In order to get a document to your Fire HD, you will have to sideload it from your PC. by connect your Fire HD to your PC through USB cord. Then just drag and drop the documents you want to transfer to the folder named " Documents" which is located on the Fire or Kindle folder under the computer folder. And you can find the document you just transfer in the Docs Library under the Local Storage.

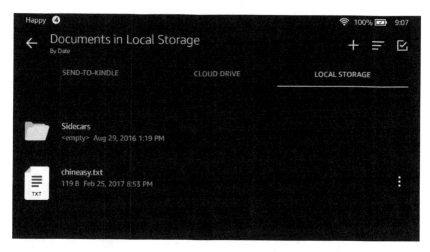

You can email it to the Kindle email address which is found in the Docs library. Because documents come in several different formats, for example, Word document will be in .doc format, they will be downloaded to your Fire HD in these formats, however, some of them will be converted to Amazon formats automatically while others will require specific software programs.

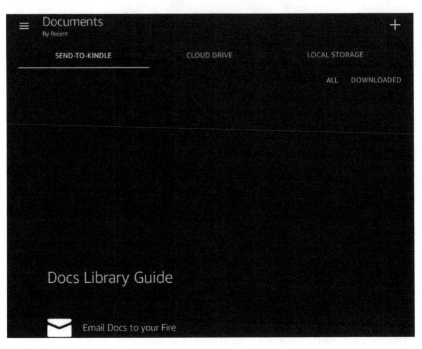

When you email a document to your Amazon email, it will automatically be uploaded to the cloud. This means that if you have a document that you do not want automatically uploaded to the cloud, you need to turn this setting off before sending it.

While you will be able to view your documents after they have been transferred to your Fire HD, you will not be able to edit them. The only way that you will be able to edit these documents is if you download an app such as OfficeSuite Pro.

Creating Folders

It is easy to create folder on your Fire HD.

1. first choose an app to get started,
2. Then you just need to press and drag the app and place it on top of other app that you want to have them in the same folder,
3. Now you will be given the option to name your folder.

You can add as many apps as you want to that folder. If you want to create another folder, just repeat the process again.

Chapter 9- When Problems Occur, Troubleshooting, Update and Reset Your Fire HD

In this chapter, I want to go over some of the basic troubleshooting techniques that you can use when you are having issues with your Fire HD. When you are troubleshooting, you will work through the most likely problems, starting with the simplest issue first.

Troubleshooting helps to reduce the cost of unneeded repair fees and it ensures that instead of spending hours on the phone with customer service, you can learn how to handle these problems on your own. Troubleshooting can seem overwhelming at first, however, you will find that it gets easier the more that you do it.

1. Keeps Turning Off

One common problem that many people face with the Fire HD is that it will turn off while it is being used.

1. The first thing that you will want to do in order to fix this is to make sure that the battery is fully charged. If the Fire HD, is turning off on its own, one of the most common reasons for this is a low battery.

 If the battery is charged, then you will want to manually turn the Fire HD off by holding the power button for about 20 seconds. After the Fire HD is off, leave it off for about one minute and then hold the power button down for 40 seconds turning it back on again.

2. If the device is not turning off but the screen is going dark, you will need to adjust your settings. In order to change your setting, go to **Settings>Display>Display Sleep**. After you have reached this location, you will want to increase the amount of time that it takes for your screen to time out.

3. Check to see if the Fire HD feels hot. Sometimes, if you have a case on or have been using it for a long time, it can get overheated. Take the case off and turn it off. Set the Fire HD to the side and let it sit for a while until it cools off. Once the Fire HD had cooled, turn it back on and see if the problem is fixed.

4. Check to make sure that your charger and your cable are working properly. Try changing the charger as well as the cord and see if this fixes the problem. I stated earlier that you have to be very careful when you are plugging in and unplugging your charger because you can ruin the cord.

If this happens, the Fire HD will not work properly and even if you are using it while it is charging, could turn off in the middle of use.

5. The last troubleshooting option that you have is to backup all of your data and then do a factory reset. In order to perform a factory, preset, go to settings>Device Option>reset to factory defaults and then choose reset.

← **Device Options**

Change Your Device Name
Happy

Battery: 63%

Date & Time

Alexa
Hold down the Home button to access Alexa on your Fire tablet.

Find Your Tablet
Allows you to remotely locate your Fire tablet.

Backup & Restore
Manage backup setting or back up your Fire now.

System Updates

Reset to Factory Defaults
Remove all personal data and downloaded content from your Fire.

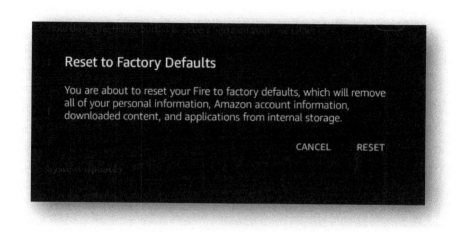

If none of this works, you will need to call the Amazon customer service.

2. Keyboard Types Erratically

Another issue that some Fire HD users have reported is that when they are using the Fire HD, it will skip letters that you are typing, type random characters, delete words, or skip pages when you are reading.

1. The first thing that you will want to do if you are dealing with this problem is to clean the screen. When you are cleaning the screen on your Fire HD, you will want to use a microfiber cloth. You will also want to make sure that if you are using a case on your Fire HD that it is fitted properly.

Finally, you will want to make sure that if you are using a screen protector, there are no bubbles underneath it.

2. You can also try turning off the Fire HD. Hold the power button down for 20 seconds, then allow the Fire HD to sit for 1 minute and then turn it back on. If this does not work, check to make sure that the battery is charged.

3. If none of this helps, you will want to backup all of your data and then do a factory reset. In order to perform a factory, preset, go to settings>Device Option>reset to factory defaults and then choose reset. If the problem persists, you will need to call Amazon customer service.

3. Internal Error Code

Some of the Fire HD users have reported that 'Internal Error' pops up on their screen while they are using their Fire HD. This code usually pops up when the user is using an App. This is usually followed by another message stating that the error is caused by network connectivity issues.

1. Begin by turning your router off, unplug it and count to 20. Plug the router back in and then turn it back on. Allow your Fire HD to connect to the network and try again.

2. Another option is to swipe down from the top of your screen and choose **Apps and Games**. Then go to **Manage All Applications**, go to **Downloaded section** and find the app that you are having problems loading. Tap on that app-and then **tap force stop.** Finally, **tap clear data and then tap okay**.

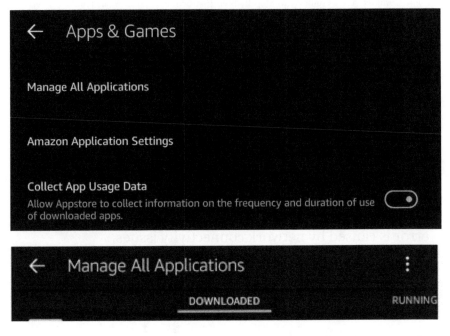

3. Make sure that the date and time are set properly. I stated earlier in this book how important it was to make sure that you set the date and time properly when you were setting up the Fire HD because it would affect your network connectivity later on.

In order to change your date and time, simply swipe down from the top of the screen and choose setting. Next, choose Device Options, then Date and Time.

Kindle Fire HD 8 & 10 User Guide:

The Complete User Guide With Step-by-Step Instructions. Master Your Kindle Fire HD 8 & 10 in 1 Hour!

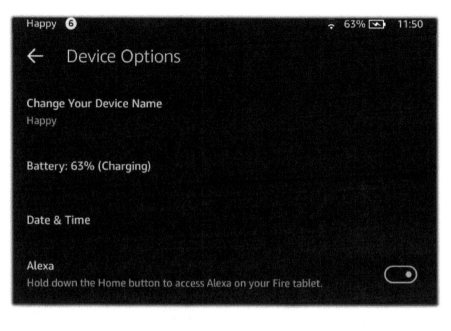

4. Try deregistering then reregistering your Fire HD. Begin by swiping down from the top of your screen, choose setting than choose my account. Next, you will choose to deregister. Once this is done, reregister.

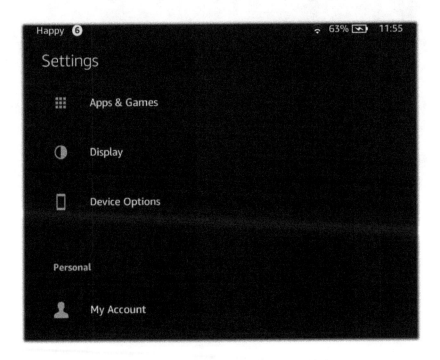

4. Can't Connect To PC

There have been reports that some customers have not been able to get their Fire HD to connect to their PC. If you are trying to transfer music, videos or documents, you may choose to do so by connecting your Fire HD to your PC. However, sometimes you might find that you are getting a message telling you that the device is not responding or that it has been disconnected. You might find that when you are looking for a file under 'computer' that you are not able to find the Fire or Kindle, which means that you have nowhere to drop the files that you are trying to transfer.

You can work around this issue by using a drop box in order to transfer your files. Or, you can email them to yourself. However, if you do not want to work around the issue, there are a few things that you can try.

1. Begin by turning off your Fire HD as well as your computer. Let both of them set for up to one minute before turning them on again. When you turn them on, you want to make sure that they are already connected via the micro-USB cable that came with your Fire HD.

2. You can also try using a different USB cord. These cords are very sensitive and many times, if something is not working between your computer and the Fire HD, the cord may be to blame.

3. Try using a different USB port on your computer and see if this helps. If none of this helps, you will want to backup your data and do a factory reset, however, if this does not fix the problem you will need to contact Amazon customer service.

5. Blue or Purple Haze Around the Edges of the Screen

Some people have reported that when they turn their Fire HD on, there is a blue or purple haze that appears at the edges of the screen making it very difficult to use the Fire HD. If this happens to you, there is nothing that you can do about it, however, Amazon will replace your Fire HD because it is a manufacturing issue.

If this occurs, you can call Amazon customer service.

It is, however, important for you to know that there is going to be a bit of blue light around the outside edge of the Fire HD due to the blue LEDs that are used, however, this is completely different from the blue/purple haze.

6. Fire HD is Overheating

I talked a little bit about the Fire HD overheating earlier, but, that was in reference to another issue. I want to talk about an issue that many people are dealing with when they are playing games or watching videos.

If this is an issue, the first thing that you want to do is to remove the case. It is important for you to understand that all devices are going to get warm, what I am talking about is when they become uncomfortably hot or that it is shutting down while you are using it.

It is possible that an app that you have recently installed is causing the issue so the first thing that you want to do is to check and see if this issue started after you installed a specific app. If this is the case, you are going to have to have to uninstall the apps. If the problem was caused by an app that you downloaded, then this will fix the issue.

However, if the issue continues, you will want to backup your data and do a factory reset to see if this solves the problem, if not, you need to contact Amazon.

7. Email is Not Updating or is Not Working

Some users have reported that they have had issues with their email not working on their Fire HD. Some have reported that they have not been able to ever get the email to work while others have reported that it will work for a short period of time and then stop working.

This is a problem that is caused by the Kindle email app as many people have found that by using a third-party email app, they are able to get around the problem.

8. The Fire HD Will Not Charge

Fire HD users have reported several issues with the Fire HD battery, one of them being that the Fire HD will not charge. There are, however, a few things that you can do before you have to contact Amazon.

1. Hold down the power button for about 20 seconds, turning off the Fire HD and then plug it in and see if it will charge.

2. You should also make sure that you are using the charging cord that came with your Fire HD. Some chargers will work with the Fire HD, however, there are those that are not compatible with it.

3. Check your charger with another device and see if it is working. If the problem is with the charger which it usually is, the other device will not charge and you will have your answer.

9. No Wi-Fi Connection

There are many different reasons that your Fire HD may not connect to your Wi-Fi network. These are a few things that you can do to resolve this problem.

1. The first thing that you will want to do is to check and see if airplane mode is on, you will go to your setting and go to the wireless setting and check to see if airplane mode is on.

2. If this does not work, you do have other options. Begin by turning off the Fire HD, by holding the power button down for about 20 seconds. Then you need to go to your router, turn it off and then unplug it. Count to 30 and then plug it back in and turn it on. Once it connects to the internet, turn your Fire HD back on and see if this fixes the issue.

3. Try rebooting the device, holding the power button down for 20 seconds. Once it is off, hold the power button down again for 40 seconds, allowing it to completely reboot.

Make sure that you first backup all of your data and then do a factory reset, we talked about how to do this earlier in the chapter.

If this does not work, you are going to have to call your internet company or Amazon for help.

10. No Sound

Some customers have complained that they are unable to hear anything through the Fire HD speakers or that they cannot hear through their earbuds. If this happens, there are plenty of options.

1. The first thing that you need to do is check to ensure that the volume is not muted. Find the volume button on the top of the Fire HD and push it until the volume is turned all the way up. If you are using earbuds or a headset, make sure that it is properly plugged in.

2. Turn your Fire HD off and unplug your headset. Then turn the Fire HD back on and then check to see if the speakers are working. If the speakers are working, then you can plug the headset back in and see if they working. Sometimes, when you plug your earbuds into your Fire HD when it is asleep, it messes up the speakers.

3. If you are having a hard time with your headset, and you have a case on your Fire HD, try removing the case and then plug your headset back in. **Sometimes, even though the cases have a hole for the jack are too small and do not provide the proper connection between the Fire HD and the headset.**

There are many different things that can go wrong with your Fire HD and the truth is, this is just a few of the issues that you may face. However, as you can see, most of the time, the resolution to the issue is quite simple. When the resolution is not simply, you do have the option to contact Amazon customer service.

How To Update Your Fire HD

Update automatically:

Normally, your Fire HD will update itself automatically when it is connected to the WIFI, and you do not need to do anything.

Update manually:

If you Fire HD didn't update automatically, you can update it manually by going to **Settings > Device Options > System Updates > Check Now/Updates.**

You need to restart the Fire HD to apply the update, you will see the message display on the screen: **"installing system update"** after you restart the device, just wait for all updates are installed before you start using the Fire HD.

Reset Your Fire HD

If you are having issues with your device and you want to reset it to the factory defaults, then follow the steps below:

1.   Go To Settings.
2.   Choose Device Options, and then select "Reset to Factory Defaults"
3.   Just Tap on Reset to confirm it.

Chapter 10- Using Alexa with Fire HD

Now you can use Alexa on your Fire HD, not only to ask questions, but to search, play music, shop and more. The Alexa app which is from the Amazon app store is compatible with all Alexa enabled devices, however, if your device is not Alexa enabled, even if you have downloaded the app, Alexa will not work.

How To Set It Up

In order to use Alexa on your Fire HD, you will first have to visit that Amazon app store and download the Alexa app.

What is Alexa? Alexa is the app that you can use on your Fire HD that is the same artificial intelligence that the Echo uses. Alexa is a voice-controlled personal assistant that can help you with every area of your life. **The Fire HD is the only tablet that supports Alexa and provides you with all of the benefits of the Echo right on your tablet.**

When you have Alexa downloaded to your Fire HD, you can use commands such as "Alexa, add event to the calendar," and instead of having to manually add an event to your calendar, you are going to be able to add it with your voice.

Having Alexa on your Fire HD is going to provide you with all of the benefits that you would have if you had the Echo sitting right inside of your living room.

Alexa Hands-Free Mode

Alexa hands-free only work with Fire HD 10 (7th Generation) that has software version 5.5.0.0 or later.

Here is how to enable and disable it:

1. Go to settings
2. Select Alexa
3. Tap (The switch for Hands-Free Mode)

How Alexa Works on The Fire HD

One of the obvious benefits of having Alexa on your Kindle is the ability to automatically reorder the products that you need. For example, if you notice that you are getting low on diapers, all you have to do is tell Alexa to reorder whatever brand you are currently using. You can also track your orders by asking, "Alexa, where is my order," and Alexa will track your shipment telling you exactly where it is and when to expect it to be delivered.

When you are using an Alexa enabled device, you will work with what are called skills. Skills for Alexa are like apps for your other devices. For example, if you want to order Dominos Pizza, you will use the Dominos skill or if you need an Uber ride, you will use the Uber skill.

You can also use skills that will allow you to turn your lights on and off, dim them, start your dryer and even preheat your oven. On top of this, you can use the Alexa app to control your television, search for your favorite television shows and increase your productivity.

The great thing about the Alexa app, however, is that it is going to allow you to use Alexa in the same way that you would use the Echo, which means that you are going to get all of the same benefits.

In order to activate Alexa, you are going to have to hold the home button down until a blue line appears across your screen. The Echo will wake with a wake word which is Alexa, however, when you are using the app on your Fire HD, Alexa will not wake with the wake word. Instead, you have to long hold the home button on your Fire HD.

If you want to turn Alexa off, which is a very good idea when your children are using it, swipe down from the top of the Fire HD screen and choose the settings option, next, you will choose the device options setting and then the Alexa app. Switch it off.

← Device Options

Change Your Device Name
navy's Fire

Battery: 9%

Date & Time

Alexa
Hold down the Home button to access Alexa on your Fire tablet.

Find Your Tablet
Allows you to remotely locate your Fire tablet.

The good news is that if you have any parental controls turned on while one of your children are using the Fire HD, Alexa is automatically shut off. Why is this important? Well, recently in the news, there was a story about a family that had an Echo in their home. They also had a little girl who was having a conversation about a dollhouse and cookies.

← Parental Controls

Household Profiles
Manage profile settings for child profiles in Household.

Parental Controls
Set a password to restrict purchasing, content types, web browsing, and access to other features. Access to Alexa is blocked when Parental Controls are enabled.

Change Password
Change Parental Controls Password.

Restrict Access for This Profile

Amazon Content and Apps
Blocked: Alexa, Web Browser, Email, Contacts, Calendars, Camera
Unblocked: Amazon Video, Newsstand, Apps & Games, Docs, Amazon Maps, Books, Photos, Audiobooks

Weeks later, a huge dollhouse and 2 pounds of cookies arrived at the front door. It is for this reason that when your children are using the Fire HD, it is important for you to either turn off the Alexa feature or to turn on parental controls.

Shopping With Alexa

Amazon users that have a 1 click payment method set up can use Alexa to help them make purchases over Amazon.com. You can also set it up so that you will need to enter a four-digit passcode in order to complete a purchase when using the Alexa app.

You will need to go to alexa.amazon.com and then go to the settings for your account. Here you will choose purchasing settings and go through these settings to determine how you want purchases to be made, for example, there is an option to allow voice purchasing.

Kindle Fire HD 8 & 10 User Guide:

The Complete User Guide With Step-by-Step Instructions. Master Your Kindle Fire HD 8 & 10 in 1 Hour!

Settings

Accounts

Notifications

Music & Media

Flash Briefing

Sports Update

Traffic

Calendar

Lists

Voice Purchasing

Household Profile

Settings

Voice Purchasing

Purchase by voice

Enable purchasing on Amazon by voice on your Alexa-enabled device.

Purchasing requires valid 1-Click payment methods. View payment settings

Voice code

A voice code helps control who is allowed to make purchases on your Alexa devices. All speakers must give the code before every purchase.

When you use Alexa to search for something via the internet on your Fire HD, your results will come from Bing and your shopping results will come from Amazon.

If you want to listen to your music, just say, "play some music" or "play the song, [title]." When you are listening to your music, you can tell Alexa to pause, go back, play and so on.

If you want to listen to a specific audio book, you will want to say, "Play (the name of the book)." The same goes for movies.

There are many different commands that you can use when it comes to Alexa and many things that you can control by using the app. If you purchase the light bulbs that work with the program, you will even be able to dim, brighten and turn your lights on or off.

You can ask Alexa for the latest news, the weather, add items to your to do list and shopping list.

Take control With Alexa on the Fire HD

On top of all of the other benefits that the Fire HD is going to provide you with, it is also going to provide you with access to Alexa which can change your life forever. By using the Alexa app, you are going to be able to take control of your life once and for all.

By using Alexa, you don't have to worry about missing appointments, being late for work because of traffic or not managing your time properly Alexa is going to help you take care of it all. If you are getting ready for work and find that you are running late, simply asking Alexa what your fastest route is will provide you not only with a traffic update but an ETA as well.

You never have to worry about running out of anything because Alexa has you covered. Instead of making a mental note of something and forgetting it later, Alexa can make a note of it and even add it to your calendar.

How to Connect Alexa to Your Calendar:

- Go to setting and click on Calendar.

- Then link your Gmail account with Alexa by input your Gmail account information.

- After you finished linking your Gmail account with Alexa, now you can return to your Alexa app and place the check mark next to what you want Alexa to access in your Gmail account. Now it's done.

- To let Alexa tell you what is your next event or your calendar by simply **say " What on my calendar? " or "What's my next event? "**

- You also can let Alexa add an event to your Gmail calendar by saying" Add an event to my calendar" then she will ask you what day, time and name of the event.

Using Alexa As Personal Assistant

Alexa is known as the perfect personal assistant because the artificial intelligence is going to help you manage every area of your life. Even helping you in the kitchen when you don't know what you are going to cook for dinner.

In order to set Alexa as a kitchen assistant, you must do the following:

- Go to the skills tab

- Search "kitchen and recipes"
- Enable the skills to let Alexa access measurements, get recipes and other information.
- Ask Alexa for the recipe that you need
- Tell Alexa what you need for that recipe and have her put it on the shopping list. By saying: add [something] to my shopping list.

It's as simple as that, and you'll be able to use Alexa to help with kitchen tasks.

There isn't much that Alexa can't do and once you use it, you will wonder how you ever lived without it. Many people struggle keeping their schedule organized, their home organized and they struggle with productivity but Alexa is the answer.

It is amazing how such a simple device such as the Kindle Fire can provide all of us with so many benefits and each person has their own favorite, but chances are that after you use the Alexa app, you are going to find that it is your favorite. After all, who doesn't want their very own personal assistant in the palm of their hands and who wouldn't want to be able to make their home, no matter how old it is the smart home of the future. Alexa is the app of the future and it is available to Fire HD users right now.

The Best Easter Eggs You Can Ask Alexa

These are commands that you can use, which most people don't know about, but that will give you a response from Alexa that you will enjoy.

Remember as you give each of these commands, you must begin hold down the home button until it turns blue, then talk to Alexa.

Top 15 Amazon Alexa Easter Eggs

1. What is the meaning of life?

2. Is there a Santa?

3. What is the best tablet?

4. Make me a sandwich.

5. What is your favorite color?

6. I am your father.

7. What is the loneliest number?

8. How much is the doggie in the window?

9. Beam me up.

10. Who's your daddy?

11. What is your quest?

12. Who is the fairest of them all?

13. To be or not to be?

14. Who ya gonna call?

15. Do you have any brothers or sisters?

Funny Music Questions

1. Alexa, Daisy Daisy.
2. Alexa, do you know the muffin man?
3. Alexa, do you really want to hurt me?
4. Alexa, Hello, It's Me.
5. Alexa, I like big butts."
6. Alexa, is this the real life?
7. Alexa, never gonna give you up
8. Alexa, sing me a song.
9. Alexa, sing me a song.
10. Alexa, twinkle, twinkle little star.
11. Alexa, what is love?
12. Alexa, what is war good for?
13. Alexa, where have all the flowers gone?
14. Alexa, who let the dogs out?
15. Alexa, who stole the cookies from the cookie jar?
16. Alexa, why do birds suddenly appear?

Asking Personal Questions with Alexa

1. Are you a robot?

2. Are you my mummy?

3. Are you tired

4. Say you're sorry.

5. Are you in love?

6. You complete me

7. Do you have any relatives?

8. Give me a kiss

9. Who loves ya, baby?

10. Who is the boss

11. Never gonna give you up.

12. Do you know Siri

13. Where do you want to be when you grow up?

14. Take me to your leader

15. Do you want to kiss?

16. Do you have a last name?

17. What is your dream job?

18. Who is your role model?

19. What is your favorite city?

20. What make you happy?

21. What is your favorite ice cream?

22. Are you human?

23. Do you have a job

24. What are you thankful for?

25. What is your favorite food?

26. Who is your daddy?

27. What can you do?

28. Why so serious?

29. Do you believe in love at first sight?

30. Do you have any brothers and sisters?

31. How tall are you?

32. Where do you live?

33. Who is your best friend?

34. Do you love me?

35. Are you smart?

36. Do you have a partner?

37. Were you sleeping?

38. How old are you?

Asking Funny Questions

1. Can you give me some money?

2. Who let the dogs out?

3. Knock Knock.

4. Party on Wayne.

5. Roll the dice.

6. Pick a random number between x and y.

7. Tell me a joke.

8. Are you lying?

9. What is the sound of one hand clapping?

10. See ya later alligator.

11. Do you like your name?

12. Are you an eavesdropping device?

13. Am I pretty?

14. Do you smoke?

15. Are you thirsty?

16. Can you see me?

17. What are you made of?

18. Why were you made?

19. I'm tired.

20. I'm hungry.

21. I'm sad.

22. You're silly.

23. Sing me a song.

24. You hurt me.

25. Ask me something.

26. Where do babies come from?

27. Say the alphabet

28. Do you have a boyfriend?

29. Do you want to fight?

30. Do you want to build a snowman?

Popular Alexa Health and Fitness Skills

Relaxing Sounds: Spa Music

Spa Music will help you feel relaxed. Try it when you feel stressed.

Relaxing Sounds: Spa Music

Voice Games

★★★★★ 1277

TRY SAYING

"Alexa, Play Spa Music"   *"Alexa, Start Spa Music"*

The Fitbit skill

This skill is a great way for you to kick start a healthy lifestyle and help you get motivated to change the way that you are living right now.

To do this, simply do the following:

- Go to the skills tab and enable "Fitbit".
  - Then you need to link your Fitbit account with Alexa.
  - Put in your Fitbit information. Now you can start using it.

7-Minutes Workout

You are going to love this skill, it is a proven set of exercise that can improve your energy, lower your stress level and increase your metabolism. The workout just needs 7-minutes, you can tell Alexa, "Start 7-minutes workout" and it will guide you through the exercise, simple and easy.

Daily Affirmation

Need daily affirmation to help you start your day, get this "Daily Affirmation Skill", it can have a positive effect on your conscious and subconscious mind. Try it and you will love it.

Ocean Surf Sound

Ocean Surf Sounds for Sleep and Relaxation
Six Voices
★ ★ ★ ★ ★ 21

TRY SAYING

"Alexa, open Ocean Sounds"   *"Alexa, play Ocean Sounds"*

If you like ocean sounds, this skill is for you, it helps you focus and relax while working on a task.

Night Night – Light & Sound

This skill can turn on Alexa's light, say a goodnight message and then play a short music for you to relax and sleep.

Minute Meditation

This is a short, guided meditation that can help you reduce stress and relax.

Minute Meditation
learyce
★★★★★ 18

Share

TRY SAYING

"Alexa, Minute Meditation"   *"Alexa, Open Minute Meditation"*

Nutrition Label

You can use this skill to ask for nutritional information on food.

Conclusion-

As you can see, the Fire HD is unlike any other Kindle Fire that has ever been released on the market. It is an all in one device that you can use to meet all of your needs.

From checking your email to listening to all of your favorite music and watching your videos, there really is nothing that the Fire HD cannot do.

I hope that this book has helped you to understand all of the ways that you can use your Fire HD and that it has shown you that not only is the Fire HD great for reading all of your favorite Kindle books, but instead, that it is an all in one device that you can use for all of your entertainment needs.

I also hope that it has helped you to deal with any issues that you might face while you are using your Fire HD and that you have been able to see that even if you are facing a problem with your Fire HD, they are not hard to solve.

Most importantly, I hope that you enjoyed this book and that it has made using the Fire IID just a little bit easier for you.

My Other Books:

This book is going to teach you everything you need to know about the Amazon Echo so that you can start using it as soon as it arrives at your home.

You will learn:

• How to set up your Amazon Echo.
• How to Connect Echo to Google Calendar
• Amazon Echo commands.
• How To Use Echo In The Kitchen
• How the Echo can improve your productivity.
• All about the Amazon Echo Skills.
• Streaming Your Favorite Music On Echo
• Creating A Smart Home With Echo
• Amazon Echo, Troubleshooting and more

Have you ever found yourself overwhelmed with life and not knowing where to turn? If you have then mindfulness is for you.

All of us can benefit from meditation, whether you are a parent or a career person. Whether we like it or not, life is stressful, and we can all benefit from a break from the anxiety.

Kindle Fire HD 8 & 10 User Guide:

The Complete User Guide With Step-by-Step Instructions. Master Your Kindle Fire HD 8 & 10 in 1 Hour!

Jennifer N. Smith